To:

_____

By:

_____

Date:

_____

Summerside Press™
Minneapolis, MN 55438
www.summersidepress.com

Hope

Compiled by Marilyn Jansen
Cover and interior design by Lisa & Jeff Franke

Summerside Press™ is an inspirational publisher offering fresh, irresistible books to uplift the heart and engage the mind.

Printed in USA.

Hope

A *Pocket Inspirations* Book

summerside
PRESS

Eternal Hope

Hope floods my heart with delight!
Running on air, mad with life, dizzy, reeling,
Upward I mount—faith is sight, life is feeling...
I am immortal! I know it! I feel it!

MARGARET WITTER FULLER

Life is what we are alive to. It is not length
but breadth.... Be alive to...goodness,
kindness, purity, love, history, poetry, music,
flowers, stars, God, and eternal hope.

MALTBIE D. BABCOCK

He who breathes into our hearts the
heavenly hope will not deceive or fail us
when we press forward to its realization.

L. B. COWMAN

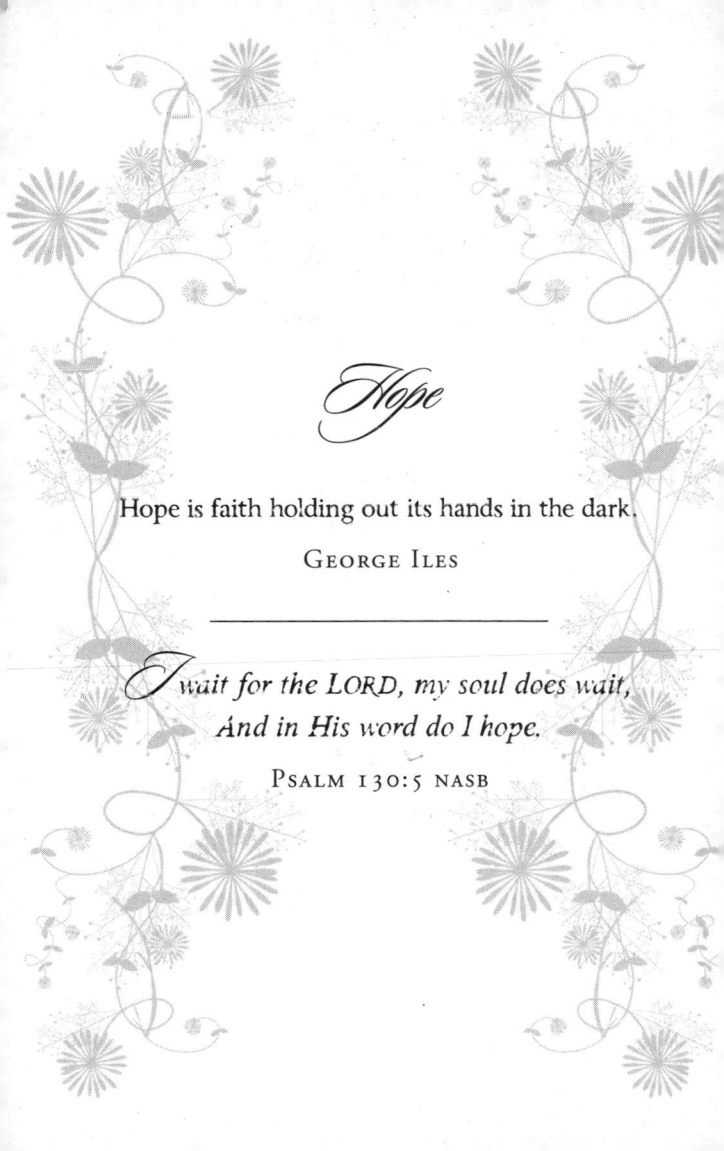

Hope

Hope is faith holding out its hands in the dark.

GEORGE ILES

---

*I wait for the LORD, my soul does wait,
And in His word do I hope.*

PSALM 130:5 NASB

Look up at all the stars in the night sky and hear your Father saying, "I carefully set each one in its place. Know that I love you more than these." Sit by the lake's edge, listening to the water lapping the shore and hear your Father gently calling you to that place near His heart.

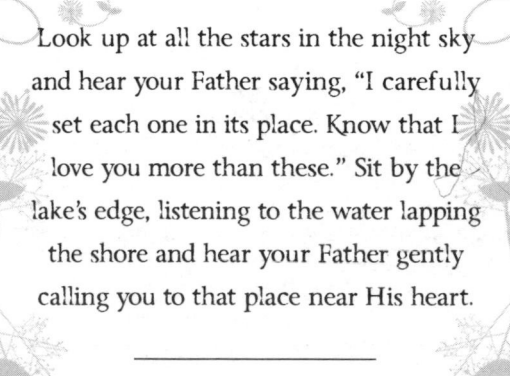

The heavens declare the glory of God, and the skies announce what his hands have made.

PSALM 19:1 NCV

Treasure in Nature

If we are children of God, we have a
tremendous treasure in nature and will
realize that it is holy and sacred. We will
see God reaching out to us in every wind
that blows, every sunrise and sunset,
every cloud in the sky, every flower that
blooms, and every leaf that fades.

OSWALD CHAMBERS

The longer I live, the more my
mind dwells upon the beauty
and the wonder of the world.

JOHN BURROUGHS

For I am bound with fleshly bands,
Joy, beauty, lie beyond my scope;
I strain my heart, I stretch my hands,
And catch at hope.

CHRISTINA ROSSETTI

Joy is the echo of God's life within us.

Be joyful. Grow to maturity.
Encourage each other. Live in
harmony and peace. Then the God
of love and peace will be with you.

2 CORINTHIANS 13:11 NLT

Joy Is

Joy is the touch of God's finger. The
object of our longing is not the touch
but the Toucher. This is true of all good
things—they are all God's touch. Whatever
we desire, we are really desiring God.

PETER KREEFT

Joy is really a road sign pointing us
to God. Once we have found God...
we no longer need to trouble ourselves
so much about the quest for joy.

C. S. LEWIS

A joyful heart is like a sunshine
of God's love, the hope of eternal
happiness, a burning flame of God.

MOTHER TERESA

"Blessed are the pure in heart for they shall see God." Meaning? They will see God work. They will see Him in their lives. They will feel His presence.

CHARLES R. SWINDOLL

God wants us to be present where we are. He invites us to see and to hear what is around us and, through it all, to discern the footprints of the Holy.

RICHARD J. FOSTER

If I rise on the wings of the dawn,
if I settle on the far side of the sea,
even there your hand will guide me,
your right hand will hold me fast.

PSALM 139:9–10 NIV

His Presence

Got may not provide us with a perfectly
ordered life, but what He does provide is
Himself, His presence, and open doors
that bring us closer to being productive,
positive, and realistic Christians.

JUDITH BRILES

Know by the light of faith that God is
present, and be content with directing
all your actions toward Him.

BROTHER LAWRENCE

When God finds a soul that rests in Him
and is not easily moved...to this same
soul He gives the joy of His presence.

CATHERINE OF GENOA

You have a unique message to deliver,
a unique song to sing, a unique act of
love to bestow. This message, this song,
and this act of love have been entrusted
exclusively to the one and only you.

JOHN POWELL

Savor little glimpses of God's
goodness and His majesty,
thankful for the gift of them.

*Isn't everything you have and
everything you are sheer gifts from God?*

1 CORINTHIANS 4:7 *THE MESSAGE*

A Splendid Gift

This bright, new day, complete with
twenty-four hours of opportunities,
choices, and attitudes comes with a
perfectly matched set of 1440 minutes.
This unique gift, this one day, cannot
be exchanged, replaced or refunded.
Handle with care. Make the most of
it. There is only one to a customer!

Live your life while you have
it. Life is a splendid gift—there
is nothing small about it.

FLORENCE NIGHTINGALE

All that we have and are is one of the
unique and never-to-be repeated ways
God has chosen to express Himself in
space and time. Each of us, made in His
image and likeness, is yet another promise
He has made to the universe that He
will continue to love it and care for it.

BRENNAN MANNING

God created human beings
in his own image. In the image
of God he created them; male
and female he created them.

GENESIS 1:27 NLT

In His Image

Leave behind your fear and dwell on
the lovingkindness of God, that you
may recover by gazing on Him.

You are a little less than angels, crown
of creation, image of God. Each person
is a revelation, a transfiguration, a
waiting for Him to manifest himself.

EDWARD FARRELL

God's designs regarding you, and
His methods of bringing about
these designs, are infinitely wise.

JEANNE GUYON

What matters supremely is not the fact that I know God, but the larger fact which underlies it—the fact that He knows me. I am graven on the palms of His hands. I am never out of His mind. All my knowledge of Him depends on His sustained initiative in knowing me. I know Him because He first knew me, and continues to know me.

J. I. Packer

I press on so that I may lay hold of that for which also I was laid hold of by Christ Jesus.

Philippians 3:12 NASB

What Matters

The God who created, names, and
numbers the stars in the heavens also
numbers the hairs of my head.... He pays
attention to very big things and to very
small ones. What matters to me matters
to Him, and that changes my life.

ELISABETH ELLIOT

What really matters is what
happens in us, not to us.

JAMES KENNEDY

One hundred years from today your
present income will be inconsequential.
One hundred years from now it won't
matter if you got that big break.... It will
greatly matter that you knew God.

DAVID SHIBLEY

Dear Lord...shine through me, and be so in me that every soul I come in contact with may feel Your presence in my soul.... Let me thus praise You in the way You love best, by shining on those around me.

JOHN HENRY NEWMAN

Nothing between us and God, our faces shining with the brightness of his face...our lives gradually becoming brighter and more beautiful as God enters our lives and we become like him.

2 CORINTHIANS 3:18 *THE MESSAGE*

Shining Through

As a countenance is made beautiful by the
soul's shining through it, so the world is
beautiful by the shining through it of God.

FREDERICH HEINRICH JACOBI

Don't ever let yourself get so busy that
you miss those little but important
extras in life—the beauty of a day, the
smile of a friend, the serenity of a quiet
moment alone. For it is often life's smallest
pleasures and gentlest joys that make
the biggest and most lasting difference.

Someone said to me once that we can see
the features of God in a single smile. Look
for that smile in the people you meet.

CHRISTOPHER DE VINCK

The Lord God loves you. He
says to you, "Behold, I make all
things new. Yes, even you!"

BASILEA SCHLINK

Lord, help me to spread Your fragrance
everywhere I go, and may Your
radiant light be visible through me.

————————

LORD, you are our Father.
We are the clay, and you are the potter.
We are all formed by your hand.

ISAIAH 64:8 NLT

New Light

I cannot open mine eyes,
But Thou art ready there to catch
My morning soul, and sacrifice....
Teach me Thy love to know;
That this new light, which now I see,
May both the work and Workman show:
Then by a sunbeam I will climb to Thee.

GEORGE HERBERT

When we allow God the privilege of
shaping our lives, we discover new depths
of purpose and meaning. What a joyful
thought to realize you are a chosen vessel
for God—perfectly suited for His use.

JONI EARECKSON TADA

If God is present at every point in space, if we cannot go where He is not, cannot even conceive of a place where He is not, why then has not that Presence become the one unanswerably celebrated fact of the world?... People do not know if God is here. What a difference it would make if they knew.

A. W. TOZER

From everlasting to everlasting, thou art God.

PSALM 90:2 KJV

All Is Well

A living, loving God can and does make
His presence felt, can and does speak to
us in the silence of our hearts, can and
does warm and caress us till we no longer
doubt that He is near, that He is here.

BRENNAN MANNING

Am I not present everywhere,
whether seen or unseen?

JEREMIAH 23:24 *THE MESSAGE*

Before me, even as behind,
God is, and all is well.

JOHN GREENLEAF WHITTIER

It is God's knowledge of me, His careful
husbanding of the ground of my being,
His constant presence in the garden of
my little life that guarantees my joy.

W. PHILLIP KELLER

We are never more fulfilled than
when our longing for God is met
by His presence in our lives.

BILLY GRAHAM

_My Presence will go with
you, and I will give you rest._

EXODUS 33:14 NIV

God With Us

God gets down on His knees among
us; gets on our level and shares
Himself with us. He does not reside
afar off and send diplomatic messages.
He kneels among us.... God shares
Himself generously and graciously.

EUGENE PETERSON

You are in the Beloved...therefore
infinitely dear to the Father,
unspeakably precious to Him. You are
never, not for one second, alone.

NORMAN DOWTY

God bless you and utterly satisfy
your heart...with Himself.

AMY CARMICHAEL

Nothing is more exciting and rewarding
than the sudden flash of insight that
leaves you a changed person.

Sir Arthur Gordon

Every day we live is a priceless gift of
God, loaded with possibilities to learn
something new, to gain fresh insights.

Dale Evans Rogers

---

*So let us know; let us press
on to know the LORD.... He will
come to us like the rain, like the
spring rain watering the earth.*

Hosea 6:3 NASB

Fresh Insights

With God, life is eternal—both in
quality and length. There is no joy
comparable to the joy of discovering
something new from God, about God.
If the continuing life is a life of joy,
we will go on discovering, learning.

EUGENIA PRICE

This life is not all. It is an "unfinished
symphony"...with those who know
that they are related to God and have
felt the power of an endless life.

HENRY WARD BEECHER

Every one of us as human beings is known and loved by the Creator apart from every other human on earth.

JAMES DOBSON

You are valuable just because you exist. Not because of what you do or what you have done, but simply because you are. Just think about the way Jesus honors you...and smile.

MAX LUCADO

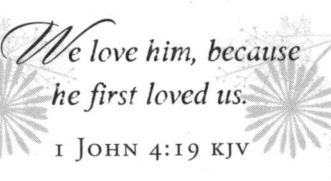

We love him, because he first loved us.

1 JOHN 4:19 KJV

Completely Loved

I pray that God, the source of hope,
will fill you completely with joy and
peace because you trust in him. Then
you will overflow with confident hope
through the power of the Holy Spirit.

ROMANS 15:13 NLT

We are of such value to God that He
came to live among us...and to guide
us home. He will go to any length
to seek us.... We can only respond
by loving God for His love.

CATHERINE OF SIENA

Use what talents you possess: the woods
would be very silent if no birds sang
there except those that sang best.

HENRY VAN DYKE

God gives everyone a special gift
and a special place to use it.

---

*Every good and perfect gift is from
above, coming down from the Father
of the heavenly lights, who does
not change like shifting shadows.*

JAMES 1:17 NIV

Special Gifts

Every person ever created is so special
that their presence in the world makes it
richer and fuller and more wonderful than
it could ever have been without them.

Where you are right now is God's
place for you. Live and obey and
love and believe right there.

1 CORINTHIANS 7:17 *THE MESSAGE*

We were not sent into this world
to do anything into which we
cannot put our hearts.

JOHN RUSKIN

There is plenitude in God.... God
is a vast reservoir of blessing
who supplies us abundantly.

EUGENE PETERSON

In difficulties, I can drink freely of
God's power and experience His touch
of refreshment and blessing—much
like an invigorating early spring rain.

*In the proper season I will
send the showers they need. There
will be showers of blessing.*

EZEKIEL 34:26 NLT

Showers of Blessings

The sun...in its full glory, either at rising
or setting—this, and many other like
blessings we enjoy daily; and for the most
of them, because they are so common,
most men forget to pay their praises.
But let not us.

Izaak Walton

God, who is love—who is, if I may say it
this way, made out of love—simply cannot
help but shed blessing on blessing upon us.

Hannah Whitall Smith

When God has become...our refuge and
our fortress, then we can reach out to
Him in the midst of a broken world and
feel at home while still on the way.

HENRI J. M. NOUWEN

My soul, wait in silence
for God only,
For my hope is from Him....
On God my salvation and my glory rest;
The rock of my strength,
my refuge is in God.

PSALM 62:5, 7 NASB

God Is Our Refuge

When you accept the fact that
sometimes seasons are dry and times
are hard and that God is in control
of both, you will discover a sense
of divine refuge, because the hope
then is in God and not in yourself.

CHARLES R. SWINDOLL

Christian hope is a different sort of
thing from other kinds. The Greek word
used in the New Testament for hope
was one which in classical literature
could mean expectation of good or
bad, but was used by Christians to
mean that in which one confides,
or to which one flees for refuge.

ELISABETH ELLIOT

God is within all things, but not included;
outside all things, but not excluded, above
all things, but not beyond their reach.

GREGORY I

Because God created the Natural—
invented it out of His love and
artistry—it demands our reverence.

C. S. LEWIS

---

*But for you who revere my name,
the sun of righteousness will rise
with healing in its wings.*

MALACHI 4:2 NIV

Expectant Reverence

Live in his presence in holy reverence,
follow the road he sets out for you,
love him, serve GOD, your God,
with everything you have in you.

DEUTERONOMY 10:12-13 *THE MESSAGE*

There is a unique kind of transparence
about things and events. The world is
seen through, and no veil can conceal
God completely. So those who are
pious are ever alert to see behind the
appearance of things a trace of the
divine, and thus their attitude toward
life is one of expectant reverence.

ABRAHAM JOSHUA HESCHEL

How beautiful it is to be alive!
To wake each morn as if the Maker's grace
Did us afresh from nothingness derive.

HENRY SEPTIMUS SUTTON

This is my Father's world;
He shines in all that's fair.
In the rustling grass I hear Him pass;
He speaks to me everywhere.

MALTBIE D. BABCOCK

I am the light of the world. Whoever follows me will never walk in darkness, but will have the light of life.

JOHN 8:12 NIV

My Father's World

Above all give me grace to use these
beauties of earth without me and this
eager stirring of life within me as a means
whereby my soul may rise from creature to
Creator, and from nature to nature's God.

JOHN BAILLIE

The God who flung from His fingertips
this universe filled with galaxies and
stars, penguins and puffins...peaches
and pears, and a world full of children
made in His own image, is the God who
loves with magnificent monotony.

BRENNAN MANNING

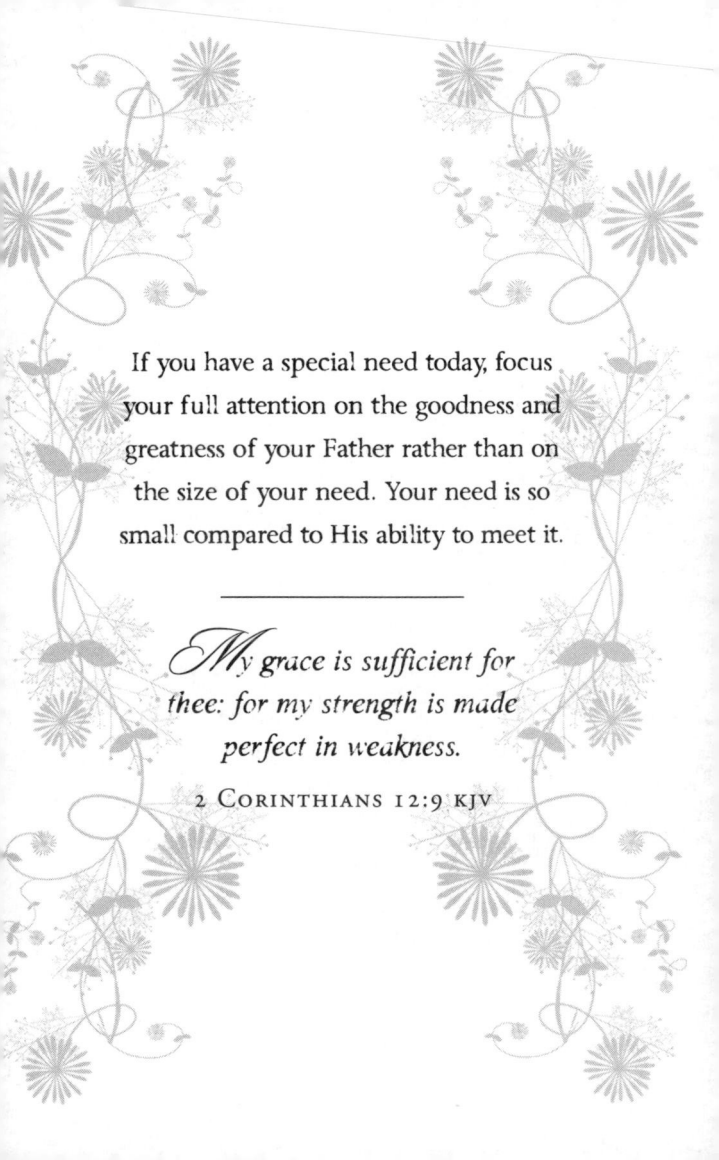

If you have a special need today, focus
your full attention on the goodness and
greatness of your Father rather than on
the size of your need. Your need is so
small compared to His ability to meet it.

---

*My grace is sufficient for
thee: for my strength is made
perfect in weakness.*

2 CORINTHIANS 12:9 KJV

Unconditional Love

There is nothing we can do that will
make God love us less, and there's
nothing we can do that will make
Him love us more. He will always
and forever love us unconditionally.
What He wants from us is that we
love Him back with all our heart.

Do not dwell upon your inner failings....
Just do this: Bring your soul to the Great
Physician—exactly as you are, even and
especially at your worst moment.... For
it is in such moments that you will most
readily sense His healing presence.

TERESA OF AVILA

Can we find a friend so faithful,
Who will all our sorrows share?
Jesus knows our every weakness:
Take it to the Lord in prayer.

GEORGE SCRIVEN

Prayer should be the key of the
day and the lock of the night.

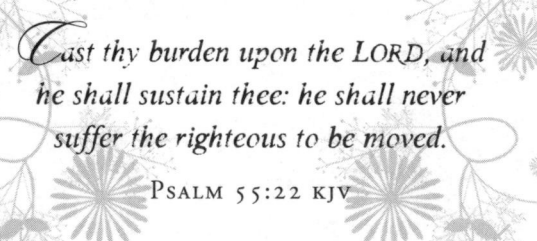

*Cast thy burden upon the LORD, and
he shall sustain thee: he shall never
suffer the righteous to be moved.*

PSALM 55:22 KJV

Everyday Prayer

Prayer is such an ordinary, everyday, mundane thing. Certainly, people who pray are no more saints than the rest of us. Rather, they are people who want to share a life with God, to love and be loved, to speak and to listen, to work and to be at rest in the presence of God.

ROBERTA BONDI

Nothing in your daily life is so insignificant and so inconsequential that God will not help you by answering your prayer.

OLE HALLESBY

Whether we are poets or parents or teachers or artists or gardeners, we must start where we are and use what we have. In the process of creation and relationship, what seems mundane and trivial may show itself to be holy, precious, part of a pattern.

Luci Shaw

I will give thanks to You, for I am fearfully and wonderfully made; wonderful are Your works, and my soul knows it very well.

Psalm 139:14 NASB

A Work of Art

Each one of us is God's special work
of art. Through us, He teaches and
inspires, delights and encourages,
informs and uplifts all those who view
our lives. God, the master artist, is most
concerned about expressing Himself—His
thoughts and His intentions—through
what He paints in our character.... [He]
wants to paint a beautiful portrait of
His Son in and through your life. A
painting like no other in all of time.

JONI EARECKSON TADA

I would rather walk with God in the
dark than go alone in the light.

MARY GARDINER BRAINARD

Heaven often seems distant and unknown,
but if He who made the road...is our
guide, we need not fear to lose the way.

HENRY VAN DYKE

*I am always with you; you
hold me by my right hand.*

PSALM 73:23 NIV

The Road Ahead

My Lord God, I have no idea where I am
going. I do not see the road ahead of
me. I cannot know for certain where it
will end.... But I believe that the desire
to please You does in fact please You.
And I hope I have that desire in all that
I am doing. I hope that I will never do
anything apart from that desire. And I
know that if I do this, You will lead me
by the right road though I may know
nothing about it.
Therefore will I trust You always though
I may seem to be lost and in the
shadow of death. I will not fear, for You
are ever with me. And You will never
leave me to face my perils alone.

THOMAS MERTON

O God, great and wonderful, who
has created the heavens, dwelling
in the light and beauty of it...teach
me to praise You, even as the lark
which offers her song at daybreak.

ISIDORE OF SEVILLE

---

*Then your light will break forth
like the dawn, and your healing will
quickly appear; then your righteousness
will go before you, and the glory of
the LORD will be your rear guard.*

ISAIAH 58:8 NIV

Praise Him

When morning gilds the skies,
My heart awakening cries:
May Jesus Christ be praised!

JOSEPH BARNBY

Does not all nature around me praise
God? If I were silent, I should be an
exception to the universe. Does not
the thunder praise Him as it rolls like
drums in the march of the God of
armies? Do not the mountains praise
Him when the woods upon their
summits wave in adoration? Does
not the lightning write His name in
letters of fire? Has not the whole earth
a voice? And shall I, can I, silent be?

C. H. SPURGEON

Whatever happens, do not lose hold of the two main ropes of life—hope and faith.

Now faith is being sure of what we hope for and certain of what we do not see.... By faith we understand that the universe was formed at God's command, so that what is seen was not made out of what was visible.... And without faith it is impossible to please God, because anyone who comes to him must believe that he exists and that he rewards those who earnestly seek him.

HEBREWS 11:1, 3, 6 NIV

Faith

Faith, as the Bible defines it, is present-
tense action. Faith means being sure
of what we hope for...now. It means
knowing something is real, this
moment, all around you, even when
you don't see it. Great faith isn't the
ability to believe long and far into the
misty future. It's simply taking God at
His word and taking the next step.

JONI EARECKSON TADA

Optimism is the faith that leads to
achievement. Nothing can be done
without hope and confidence

HELEN KELLER

With kindness, the difficult becomes easy, the obscure clear; life assumes a charm and its miseries are softened. If we knew the power of kindness, we should transform this world into a paradise.

WAGNER

Love is the only force capable of transforming an enemy into a friend.

MARTIN LUTHER KING JR.

_____

Create in me a clean heart, O God; and renew a right spirit within me.

PSALM 51:10 KJV

A Life Transformed

To pray is to change. This is a great grace. How good of God to provide a path whereby our lives can be taken over by love and joy and peace and patience and kindness and goodness and faithfulness and gentleness and self-control.

RICHARD J. FOSTER

For God is, indeed, a wonderful Father who longs to pour out His mercy upon us, and whose majesty is so great that He can transform us from deep within.

TERESA OF AVILA

A life transformed by the power of God is always a marvel and a miracle.

GERALDINE NICHOLAS

The meaning of earthly existence lies, not as
we have grown used to thinking, in prospering,
but in the development of the soul.

ALEKSANDR SOLZHENITSYN

Service is the rent we each pay for living.
It is not something to do in your spare
time; it is the very purpose of life.

MARIAN WRIGHT EDELMAN

*We know that all things work together
for good to them that love God, to them who
are the called according to his purpose.*

ROMANS 8:28 KJV

A Life of Purpose

Happiness is living by inner
purpose, not by outer pressures.

DAVID AUGSBERGER

Have a purpose in life, and having it,
throw into your work such strength of
mind and muscle as God has given you.

THOMAS CARLYLE

The patterns of our days are always
rearranging...and each design for living is
unique, graced with its own special beauty.

The purpose of life is a life of purpose.

ROBERT BYRNE

An infinite God can give all of Himself
to each of His children. He does not
distribute Himself that each may have
a part, but to each one He gives all of
Himself as fully as if there were no
others.... His love has not changed. It
hasn't cooled off, and it needs no increase
because He has already loved us with
infinite love and there is no way that
infinitude can be increased.... He is the
same yesterday, today, and forever!

A. W. TOZER

———————

*Take a long, hard look. See how great
he is—infinite, greater than anything
you could ever imagine or figure out!*

JOB 36:26 *THE MESSAGE*

Infinite Love

At the very heart and foundation of all
God's dealings with us, however dark
and mysterious they may be, we must
dare to believe in and assert the infinite,
unmerited, and unchanging love of God.

L. B. COWMAN

Everything which relates to God is
infinite. We must therefore, while we
keep our hearts humble, keep our
aims high. Our highest services are
indeed but finite, imperfect. But as
God is unlimited in goodness, He
should have our unlimited love.

HANNAH MORE

Contentment is not the fulfillment
of what you want, but the realization
of how much you already have.

---

*I have learned to be content in
whatever circumstances I am. I
know how to get along with humble
means, and I also know how to
live in prosperity; in any and every
circumstance I have learned the secret
of being filled and going hungry,
both of having abundance and
suffering need. I can do all things
through Him who strengthens me.*

PHILIPPIANS 4:11–13 NASB

Contentment

If we are cheerful and contented, all
nature smiles...the flowers are more
fragrant, the birds sing more sweetly, and
the sun, moon, and stars all appear more
beautiful, and seem to rejoice with us.

ORISON SWETT MARDEN

Godliness with contentment is great
gain. For we brought nothing into the
world, and we can take nothing out
of it. But if we have food and clothing,
we will be content with that.

1 TIMOTHY 6:6–8 NIV

This life is not all. It is an "unfinished symphony"...with him who knows that he is related to God and has felt "the power of an endless life."

HENRY WARD BEECHER

As we grow in our capacities to see and enjoy the joys that God has placed in our lives, life becomes a glorious experience of discovering His endless wonders.

I will show wonders in the heavens and on the earth.

JOEL 2:30 NIV

Endless Wonders

Little drops of water,
Little grains of sand,
Make the mighty ocean
And the pleasant land.
Little deeds of kindness,
Little words of love,
Help to make earth happy
Like the heaven above.

JULIA FLETCHER CARNEY

Strength, rest, guidance, grace, help,
sympathy, love—all from God to
us! What a list of blessings!

EVELYN STENBOCK

Live for today but hold your hands
open to tomorrow. Anticipate the future
and its changes with joy. There is a
seed of God's love in every event, every
circumstance, every unpleasant situation
in which you may find yourself.

BARBARA JOHNSON

———————

The joy of the LORD is your strength.

NEHEMIAH 8:10 KJV

Made for Joy

Our hearts were made for joy. Our
hearts were made to enjoy the One
who created them. Too deeply planted
to be much affected by the ups and
downs of life, this joy is a knowing and
a being known by our Creator. He sets
our hearts alight with radiant joy.

WENDY MOORE

If one is joyful, it means that one is
faithfully living for God, and that nothing
else counts; and if one gives joy to
others one is doing God's work. With
joy without and joy within, all is well.

JANET ERSKINE STUART

Life in the presence of God should be known
to us in conscious experience. It is a life to
be enjoyed every moment of every day.

A. W. TOZER

---

*Many, O LORD my God, are the wonders
which You have done,
And Your thoughts toward us;
There is none to compare with You
If I would declare and speak of them,
They would be too numerous to count.*

PSALM 40:10 NASB

In God's Thoughts

Tonight I will sleep beneath Your feet, O
Lord of the mountains and valleys, ruler
of the trees and vines. I will rest in Your
love, with You protecting me as a father
protects his children, with You watching
over me as a mother watches over her
children. Then tomorrow the sun will
rise and I will not know where I am; but
I know that You will guide my footsteps.

EARLY AMERICAN PRAYER

We have been in God's thought from
all eternity, and in His creative love,
His attention never leaves us.

MICHAEL QUOIST

The reason for loving God is God Himself,
and the measure in which we should
love Him is to love Him without measure.

BERNARD OF CLAIRVAUX

---

*May God himself, the God who
makes everything holy and whole,
make you holy and whole, put you
together—spirit, soul, and body—and
keep you fit for the coming of our
Master, Jesus Christ. The One who
called you is completely dependable.*

1 THESSALONIANS 5:23–24 *THE MESSAGE*

Himself

Although it is good to think upon the kindness of God, and to love Him and worship Him for it, it is far better to gaze upon the pure essence of Him and to love Him and worship Him for Himself.

We desire many things, and God offers us only one thing. He can offer us only one thing—Himself. He has nothing else to give. There is nothing else to give.

PETER KREEFT

Within each of us there is an inner place
where the living God Himself longs to
dwell, our sacred center of belief.

I will remember that when I give Him my
heart, God chooses to live within me—body
and soul. And I know He really is as close as
breathing, His very Spirit inside of me.

I pray that out of his glorious riches
he may strengthen you with power
through his Spirit in your inner being.

EPHESIANS 3:16 NIV

An Inner Place

Retire from the world each day to some private
spot.... Stay in the secret place till the surrounding
noises begin to fade out of your heart and a
sense of God's presence envelops you.... Listen
for the inward Voice till you learn to recognize
it.... Give yourself to God and then be what
and who you are without regard to what others
think.... Learn to pray inwardly every moment.

A.W. TOZER

No one can get inner peace by pouncing on
it, by vigorously willing to have it. Peace is
a margin of power around our daily need.
Peace is a consciousness of springs too
deep for earthly droughts to dry up.

HARRY EMERSON FOSDICK

The grace of God means something
like: Here is your life. You might never
have been, but you are because the party
wouldn't have been complete without you.

FREDERICK BUECHNER

Grace and gratitude belong together like
heaven and earth. Grace evokes gratitude
like the voice an echo. Gratitude follows
grace as thunder follows lightning.

KARL BARTH

*God is sheer mercy and grace;
not easily angered, he's rich in love....
As far as sunrise is from sunset, he
has separated us from our sins.*

PSALM 103:8, 12 *THE MESSAGE*

Nothing but Grace

There is nothing but God's grace.
We walk upon it; we breathe it;
we live and die by it; it makes the
nails and axles of the universe.

ROBERT LOUIS STEVENSON

Grace is no stationary thing, it is ever
becoming. It is flowing straight out
of God's heart. Grace does nothing
but re-form and convey God. Grace
makes the soul conformable to the
will of God. God, the ground of the
soul, and grace go together.

JOHANNES ECKHART

What makes life worthwhile is having
a big enough objective, something
which catches our imagination and lays
hold of our allegiance.... What higher,
more exalted, and more compelling
goal can there be than to know God?

J. I. PACKER

———————————

*I consider everything a loss
compared to the surpassing greatness
of knowing Christ Jesus my Lord.*

PHILIPPIANS 3:8 NIV

A Life Worthwhile

I wish you humor and a twinkle in the eye. I wish you glory and the strength to bear its burdens. I wish you sunshine on your path and storms to season your journey. I wish you peace—in the world in which you live and in the smallest corner of the heart where truth is kept. I wish you faith—to help define your living and your life. More I cannot wish you—except perhaps love—to make all the rest worthwhile.

ROBERT A. WARD

Always be in a state of expectancy,
and see that you leave room for
God to come in as He likes.

Oswald Chambers

God's hand is always there; once you
grasp it you'll never wants to let go.

———————

*How lovely are Your dwelling
places, O LORD of hosts! My soul
longed and even yearned for the
courts of the LORD; my heart and
my flesh sing for joy to the living
God.... For a day in Your courts is
better than a thousand outside.*

Psalm 84:1–2, 10 nasb

Always There

We need never shout across the
spaces to an absent God. He is
nearer than our own soul, closer
than our most secret thoughts.

A. W. TOZER

God is always present in the temple
of your heart...His home. And when
you come in to meet Him there, you
find that it is the one place of deep
satisfaction where every longing is met.

God is the sunshine that warms us,
the rain that melts away the frost
and waters the young plants. The
presence of God is a climate of strong
and bracing love, always there.

JOAN ARNOLD

Faith sees the invisible, believes the incredible, and receives the impossible.

God wants us to approach life, full of expectancy that God is going to be at work in every situation as we grow in our faith in Him.

COLIN URQUHART

Faith is not a sense, not sight, not reason, but a taking God at His Word.

EVANS

With God all things are possible.

MARK 10:27 KJV

Faith Adventure

There will always be the unknown.
There will always be the unprovable.
But faith confronts those frontiers
with a thrilling leap. Then life
becomes vibrant with adventure!

ROBERT SCHULLER

Faith means you want God and want
to want nothing else.... In faith there
is movement and development.
Each day something is new.

BRENNAN MANNING

Be joyful in hope, patient in
affliction, faithful in prayer.

ROMANS 12:12 NIV

God's pursuit of praise from us and our
pursuit of pleasure in Him are one and the
same pursuit. God's quest to be glorified
and our quest to be satisfied reach their
goal in this one experience: our delight
in God which overflows in praise.

JOHN PIPER

Earth, with her thousand
voices, praises God.

SAMUEL TAYLOR COLERIDGE

O sing unto the LORD a new song:
sing unto the LORD, all the earth.

PSALM 96:1 KJV

Overflowing Praise

All enjoyment spontaneously overflows
into praise.... The world rings with
praise...walkers praising the countryside,
players praising their favorite game....
I think we delight to praise what we
enjoy because the praise not merely
expresses but completes the enjoyment;
it is the appointed consummation.

C. S. LEWIS

Angels bright, heavens high, waters
deep, give God the praise.

CHRISTOPHER COLLINS

Our Creator would never have made such
lovely days, and given us the deep hearts to
enjoy them, above and beyond all thought,
unless we were meant to be immortal.

NATHANIEL HAWTHORNE

May your life become one of glad
and unending praise to the Lord as
you journey through this world.

TERESA OF AVILA

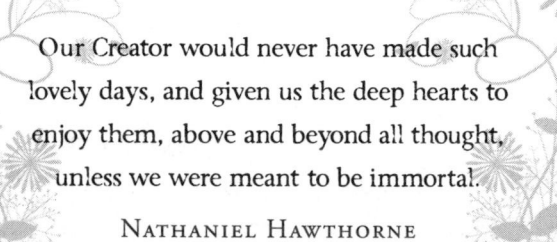

The whole earth is full of his glory.

ISAIAH 6:3 KJV

His Beautiful World

The God who holds the whole
world in His hands wraps Himself
in the splendor of the sun's light
and walks among the clouds.

Forbid that I should walk through Thy
beautiful world with unseeing eyes:
Forbid that the lure of the market-
place should ever entirely steal my
heart away from the love of the
open acres and the green trees:
Forbid that under the low roof of
workshop or office or study I should
ever forget Thy great overarching sky.

JOHN BAILLIE

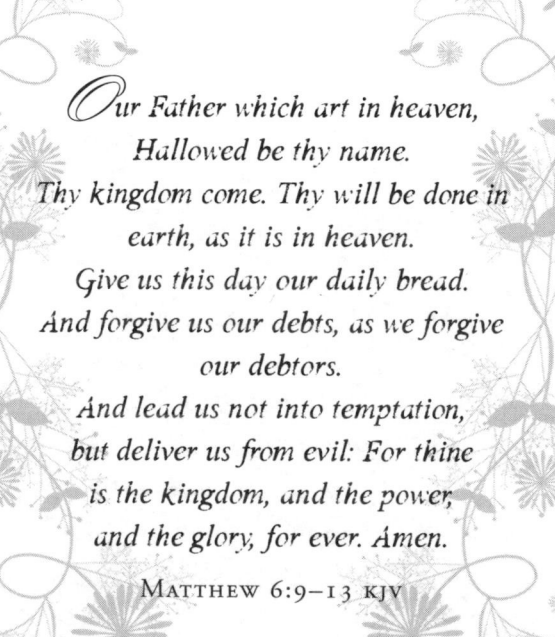

Our Father which art in heaven,
Hallowed be thy name.
Thy kingdom come. Thy will be done in
earth, as it is in heaven.
Give us this day our daily bread.
And forgive us our debts, as we forgive
our debtors.
And lead us not into temptation,
but deliver us from evil: For thine
is the kingdom, and the power,
and the glory, for ever. Amen.

MATTHEW 6:9–13 KJV

The Lord's Prayer

They who seek the throne of grace
find that throne in every place;
If we live a life of prayer, God
is present everywhere.

OLIVER HOLDEN

Part of our job is simply to be.... Part of our job is
to expect that, if we are attentive and willing, God
will "give us prayer," will give us the things we
need, "our daily bread," to heal and grow in love.

ROBERTA BONDI

If the Lord be with us, we have no cause
to fear. His eye is upon us, His arm over
us, His ear open to our prayer— His grace
sufficient, His promise unchangeable.

JOHN NEWTON

That is God's call to us—simply to be
people who are content to live close to
Him and to renew the kind of life in which
the closeness is felt and experienced.

THOMAS MERTON

The faithful love of the Lord never ends!
His mercies never cease.
Great is his faithfulness; his mercies
begin afresh each morning.

LAMENTATIONS 3:22–23 NLT

New Every Morning

Hold on, my child! Joy comes in the morning!
Weeping only lasts for the night....
The darkest hour means dawn is just in sight!

GLORIA GAITHER

O LORD, be gracious to us; we long for
you. Be our strength every morning,
our salvation in time of distress.

ISAIAH 33:2 NIV

Ah, Hope! what would life be, stripped of
thy encouraging smiles, that teach us to
look behind the dark clouds of today, for the
golden beams that are to gild the morrow.

SUSANNA MOODIE

We walk without fear, full of hope
and courage and strength to do His
will, waiting for the endless good
which He is always giving as fast as
He can get us able to take it in.

GEORGE MACDONALD

---

*Open your mouth and taste, open
your eyes and see—how good GOD
is. Blessed are you who run to him.
Worship God if you want the best;
worship opens doors to all his goodness.*

PSALM 34:8–9 *THE MESSAGE*

The Goodness of God

The goodness of God is infinitely
more wonderful than we will
ever be able to comprehend.

A. W. TOZER

All that is good, all that is true, all that is
beautiful, all that is beneficent, be it great
or small, be it perfect or fragmentary,
natural as well as supernatural, moral
as well as material, comes from God.

JOHN HENRY NEWMAN

In extravagance of soul we seek His face. In generosity of heart, we glean His gentle touch. In excessiveness of spirit, we love Him and His love comes back to us a hundredfold.

TRICIA MCCARY RHODES

Trust steadily in God, hope unswervingly, love extravagantly. And the best of the three is love.

1 CORINTHIANS 13:13 *THE MESSAGE*

A Firsthand Experience

Listening to God is a firsthand experience....
God invites *you* to vacation in His splendor.
He invites *you* to feel the touch of His
hand. He invites *you* to feast at His table.
He wants to spend time with *you*.

MAX LUCADO

Prayer is everywhere.... Prayer is
language used to respond to the most
that has been said to us, with the
potential for saying all that is in us.

EUGENE PETERSON

In both simple and eloquent ways,
our infinite God personally reveals
glimpses of Himself in the finite.

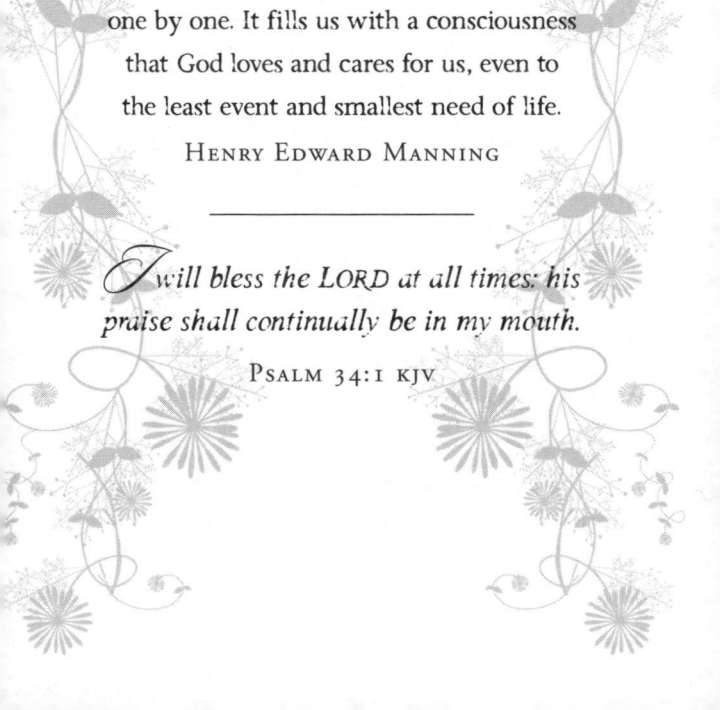

Gratitude consists in a watchful, minute
attention to the particulars of our state,
and to the multitude of God's gifts, taken
one by one. It fills us with a consciousness
that God loves and cares for us, even to
the least event and smallest need of life.

HENRY EDWARD MANNING

———————

*I will bless the LORD at all times: his
praise shall continually be in my mouth.*

PSALM 34:1 KJV

Happiness and Gratitude

Our inner happiness depends not on what
we experience but on the degree of our
gratitude to God, whatever the experience.

ALBERT SCHWEITZER

So wait before the Lord. Wait in the
stillness. And in that stillness, assurance
will come to you. You will know that
you are heard...you will hear quiet words
spoken to you yourself, perhaps to your
grateful surprise and refreshment.

AMY CARMICHAEL

It is not how much we have, but how
much we enjoy, that makes happiness.

CHARLES H. SPURGEON

Made in His image, we can have real
meaning, and we can have real knowledge
through what He has communicated to us.

FRANCIS SCHAEFFER

In the very beginning it was God who
formed us by His Word. He made us in His
own image. God was spirit and He gave us
a spirit so that He could come into us and
mingle His own life with our life.

JEANNE GUYON

*For in Him all the fullness of
Deity dwells in bodily form, and in
Him you have been made complete.*

COLOSSIANS 2:9–10 NASB

In His Likeness

The God of the universe—the One who
created everything and holds it all in His
hand—created each of us in His image, to
bear His likeness, His imprint. It is only
when Christ dwells within our hearts,
radiating the pure light of His love through
our humanity that we discover who we
are and what we were intended to be.

God's children who joyously know and claim
who they are and whose they are, will be most
likely to manifest the family likeness, just
because they know they are His children.

ALICE CHAPIN

The huge dome of the sky is...the most like infinity. When God made space and worlds that move in space, and clothed our world with air, and gave us such eyes and such imaginations as those we have, He knew what the sky would mean to us.... We cannot be certain that this was not indeed one of the chief purposes for which Nature was created.

C. S. LEWIS

The heavens declare his righteousness, and all the people see his glory.

PSALM 97:6 KJV

Glorious Handiwork

He made you so you could share
in His creation, could love and
laugh and know Him.

TED GRIFFEN

You are a creation of God unequaled
anywhere in the universe.... Thank
Him for yourself and then for all the
rest of His glorious handiwork.

NORMAN VINCENT PEALE

God's love is like a river springing up in the
Divine Substance and flowing endlessly
through His creation, filling all things
with life and goodness and strength.

THOMAS MERTON

God reads the secrets of the heart. God reads the most intimate feelings, even those which we are not aware of.

JEAN-NICHOLAS GROU

Because God is responsible for our welfare, we are told to cast all our care upon Him, for He cares for us. God says, "I'll take the burden—don't give it a thought—leave it to Me." God is keenly aware that we are dependent upon Him for life's necessities.

BILLY GRAHAM

Casting all your care upon him; for he careth for you.

1 PETER 5:7 KJV

Totally Aware

God is every moment totally aware of
each one of us. Totally aware in intense
concentration and love.... No one passes
through any area of life, happy or tragic,
without the attention of God with him.

EUGENIA PRICE

You saw how the LORD your God cared for you
all along the way as you traveled through the
wilderness, just as a father cares for his child.

DEUTERONOMY 1:31 NLT

You are God's created beauty and the
focus of His affection and delight.

JANET L. WEAVER SMITH

I believe that nothing that happens to me is meaningless, and that it is good for us all that it should be so.... As I see it, I'm here for some purpose.

DIETRICH BONHOEFFER

When the world around us staggers from lack of direction, God offers purpose, hope, and certainty.

GLORIA GAITHER

May the favor of the Lord our God rest upon us; establish the work of our hands for us.

PSALM 90:17 NIV

Destiny

Recognizing who we are in Christ and
aligning our life with God's purpose
for us gives a sense of destiny.... It
gives form and direction to our life.

JEAN FLEMING

When we live life centered around what
others like, feel, and say, we lose touch
with our own identity. I am an eternal
being, created by God. I am an individual
with purpose. It's not what I get from life,
but who I am, that makes the difference.

NEVA COYLE

God has a purpose for your life and
no one else can take your place.

God cares for the world He created, from
the rising of a nation to the falling of the
sparrow. Everything in the world lies under
the watchful gaze of His providential
eyes, from the numbering of the days
of our life to the numbering of the
hairs on our head. When we look at the
world from that perspective, it produces
within us a response of reverence.

KEN GIRE

———————————

*For He will give His angels
charge concerning you, to
guard you in all your ways.*

PSALM 91:11 NASB

Watchful Care

He paints the lily of the field,
Perfumes each lily bell;
If He so loves the little flowers,
I know He loves me well.

MARIA STRAUS

The LORD is in his holy Temple; the
LORD still rules from heaven. He watches
everything closely, examining every person
on earth.... For the righteous LORD loves
justice. The virtuous will see his face.

PSALM 11:4, 7 NLT

God's in His heaven—
All's right with the world!

ROBERT BROWNING

Sunset
The day is done,
The sun has set,
Yet light still tints the sky;
My heart stands still
In reverence,
For God is passing by.

RUTH ALLA WAGER

---

*Where morning dawns and evening
fades you call forth songs of joy.*

PSALM 65:8 NIV

God Is Passing By

Friendships, family ties, the
companionship of little children, an
autumn forest flung in prodigality against
a deep blue sky, the intricate design
and haunting fragrance of a flower, the
counterpoint of a Bach fugue or the
melodic line of a Beethoven sonata, the
fluted note of bird song, the glowing
glory of a sunset: the world is aflame
with things of eternal moment.

E. MARGARET CLARKSON

Always new. Always exciting. Always
full of promise. The mornings of our
lives, each a personal daily miracle!

GLORIA GAITHER

If God is here for us and not
elsewhere, then in fact *this place* is
holy and *this moment* is sacred.

ISABEL ANDERS

God still draws near to us in the ordinary,
commonplace, everyday experiences and
places.... He comes in surprising ways.

HENRY GARIEPY

---

*This is the day which the LORD hath
made; we will rejoice and be glad in it.*

PSALM 118:24 KJV

Simple Wonders

A fiery sunset, tiny pansies by the wayside, the sound of raindrops tapping on the roof—what an extraordinary delight to notice simple wonders! With wide eyes and full hearts, we have the opportunity to cherish what others have missed and to thank God for them.

The wonder of our Lord is that He is so accessible to us in the common things of our lives: the cup of water...breaking of the bread...welcoming children into our arms...fellowship over a meal...giving thanks. A simple attitude of caring, listening, and lovingly telling the truth.

NANCIE CARMICHAEL.

Allow your dreams a place in
your prayers and plans. God-given
dreams can help you move into the
future He is preparing for you.

Always stay connected to people and
seek out things that bring you joy.
Dream with abandon. Pray confidently.

BARBARA JOHNSON

A dream fulfilled is a tree of life.

PROVERBS 13:12 NLT

Hold Fast Your Dreams

Hold fast your dreams!
Within your heart
Keep one still, secret spot
Where dreams may go
And, sheltered so,
May thrive and grow...
O keep a place apart,
Within your heart,
For little dreams to go!

LOUISE DRISCOLL

I came so they can have real and eternal life,
more and better life than they ever dreamed of.

JOHN 10:10 *THE MESSAGE*

At every moment, God is calling your name and waiting to be found. To each cry of "Oh Lord," God answers, "I am here."

They who seek the throne of grace
Find that throne in every place;
If we live a life of prayer,
God is present everywhere.

OLIVER HOLDEN

God is our refuge and strength,
an ever-present help in trouble.
Therefore we will not fear.

PSALM 46:1–2 NIV

Ever Present

When I walk by the wayside, He is along
with me.... Amid all my forgetfulness
of Him, He never forgets me.

THOMAS CHALMERS

There's not a tint that paints the rose
Or decks the lily fair,
Or marks the humblest flower that grows,
But God has placed it there....
There's not a place on earth's vast round,
In ocean's deep or air,
Where love and beauty are not found,
For God is everywhere.

All the beautiful sentiments in the world
weigh less than a simple lovely action.

JAMES RUSSELL LOWELL

From the world we see, hear, and touch,
we behold inspired visions that reveal
God's glory. In the sun's light, we catch
warm rays of grace and glimpse His
eternal design. In the birds' song, we hear
His voice and it reawakens our desire for
Him. At the wind's touch, we feel His
Spirit and sense our eternal existence.

*Oh, worship the LORD in
the beauty of holiness!*

PSALM 96:9 NKJV

Countless Beauties

The beauty of the earth, the beauty
of the sky, the order of the stars, the
sun, the moon...their very loveliness is
their confession of God: for who made
these lovely mutable things, but He
who is Himself unchangeable beauty?

AUGUSTINE

May God give you eyes to see beauty
only the heart can understand.

All the world is an utterance
of the Almighty. Its countless
beauties, its exquisite adaptations,
all speak to you of Him.

PHILLIPS BROOKS

The Lord's chief desire is to reveal Himself to you and, in order for Him to do that, He gives you abundant grace. The Lord gives you the experience of enjoying His presence. He touches you, and His touch is so delightful that, more than ever, you are drawn inwardly to Him.

JEANNE GUYON

I am not what I ought to be, I am not what I wish to be, I am not what I hope to be; but, by the grace of God, I am not what I was.

JOHN NEWTON

Set your hope fully on the grace to be given you when Jesus Christ is revealed.

1 PETER 1:13 NIV

Grace Revealed

Look deep within yourself and recognize
what brings life and grace into your
heart. It is this that can be shared with
those around you. You are loved by
God. This is an inspiration to love.

CHRISTOPHER DE VINCK

All God's glory and beauty come from
within, and there He delights to dwell. His
visits there are frequent, His conversation
sweet, His comforts refreshing, His
peace passing all understanding.

THOMAS À KEMPIS

God listens in compassion and love, just
like we do when our children come
to us. He delights in our presence.

RICHARD J. FOSTER

Be still, and in the quiet moments, listen to the
voice of your heavenly Father. His words can
renew your spirit...no one knows you and your
needs like He does.

JANET L. WEAVER SMITH

---

*I love the LORD because he hears my voice
and my prayer for mercy.
Because he bends down to listen,
I will pray as long as I have breath!*

PSALM 116:1–2 NLT

God Listens

Open wide the windows of our spirits and
fill us full of light; open wide the door of our
hearts, that we may receive and entertain
Thee with all our powers of adoration.

CHRISTINA ROSSETTI

We know that God...listens to the
godly man who does his will.

JOHN 9:31 NIV

We come this morning—
Like empty pitchers to a full fountain,
With no merits of our own,
O Lord—open up a window of heaven,
And listen this morning.

JAMES WELDON JOHNSON

Someone speaks a word of
hope to a discouraged soul, and
light shines in his prison.

RUTH ANN POLSTON

Stand outside this evening. Look at the
stars. Know that you are special and
loved by the One who created them.

One of Jesus' specialties is to make
somebodies out of nobodies.

HENRIETTA MEARS

---

*God demonstrates His own love
toward us, in that while we were
yet sinners, Christ died for us.*

ROMANS 5:8 NASB

Someone Special

The Creator thinks enough of you
to have sent Someone very special
so that you might have life—
abundantly, joyfully, completely,
and victoriously.

When we love someone, we want to
be with them, and we view their love for
us with great honor even if they are not a
person of great status. For this reason—and
not because of our great status—God
values our love. So much, in fact, that
He suffered greatly on our behalf.

JOHN CHRYSOSTOM

God created us with an overwhelming
desire to soar.... He designed us to
be tremendously productive and "to
mount up with wings like eagles,"
realistically dreaming of what He
can do with our potential.

CAROL KENT

---

*I'll lead you to buried treasures,
secret caches of valuables—
Confirmations that it is, in fact, I,
God...who calls you by your name.*

ISAIAH 45:3 *THE MESSAGE*

Dreams Fulfilled

Lift up your eyes. Your heavenly Father
waits to bless you—in inconceivable
ways to make your life what you
never dreamed it could be.

ANNE ORTLUND

God is not an elusive dream or a
phantom to chase, but a divine
person to know. He does not avoid
us, but seeks us. When we seek Him,
the contact is instantaneous.

NEVA COYLE

The human heart has hidden treasures,
In secret kept, in silence sealed;—
The thoughts, the hopes, the
dreams, the pleasures,
Whose charms were broken if revealed.

CHARLOTTE BRONTË

Settle yourself in solitude and
you will come upon Him.

TERESA OF AVILA

We must drink deeply from the very
Source, the deep calm and peace of
interior quietude and refreshment
of God, allowing the pure water of
divine grace to flow plentifully and
unceasingly from the Source itself.

MOTHER TERESA

---

*Whoever drinks of the water
that I will give him shall never
thirst; but the water that I will give
him will become in him a well of
water springing up to eternal life.*

JOHN 4:14 NASB

Settled in Solitude

Solitude liberates us from entanglements
by carving out a space from which
we can see ourselves and our
situation before the Audience of
One. Solitude provides the private
place where we can take our bearings
and so make God our North Star.

Os Guinness

Peace with God brings the peace of God.
It is a peace that settles our nerves, fills
our mind, floods our spirit, and in the
midst of the uproar around us, gives us
the assurance that everything is all right.

Bob Mumford

God is with us in the midst of our daily, routine lives. In the middle of cleaning the house or driving somewhere in the pickup.... Often it's in the middle of the most mundane task that He lets us know He is there with us. We realize, then, that there can be no "ordinary" moments for people who live their lives with Jesus.

MICHAEL CARD

God himself shall be with them, and be their God.

REVELATION 21:3 KJV

The Sacred Ordinary

Much of what is sacred is hidden in the
ordinary, everyday moments of our lives.
To see something of the sacred in those
moments takes slowing down so we
can live our lives more reflectively.

KEN GIRE

We encounter God in the ordinariness of
life, not in the search for spiritual highs
and extraordinary, mystical experiences,
but in our simple presence in life.

BRENNAN MANNING

Simplicity will enable you to leap lightly.
Increasingly you will find yourself living in
a state of grace, finding...the sacred in the
ordinary, the mystical in the mundane.

DAVID YOUNT

God came to us because God wanted to join us
on the road, to listen to our story, and to help
us realize that we are not walking in circles but
moving toward the house of peace and joy.

HENRI J. M. NOUWEN

---

*Do not worry about anything,
but pray and ask God for everything
you need, always giving thanks. And
God's peace, which is so great we
cannot understand it, will keep your
hearts and minds in Christ Jesus.*

PHILIPPIANS 4:6-7 NCV

Enfolded in Peace

I will let God's peace infuse every part
of today. As the chaos swirls and life's
demands pull at me on all sides, I will
breathe in God's peace that surpasses
all understanding. He has promised
that He would set within me a peace
too deeply planted to be affected by
unexpected or exhausting demands.

Calm me, O Lord, as you stilled the storm,
Still me, O Lord, keep me from harm.
Let all the tumult within me cease,
Enfold me, Lord, in your peace.

CELTIC TRADITIONAL

God cannot give us a happiness and peace
apart from Himself, because it is not there.
There is no such thing.

C. S. LEWIS

Everyone has a unique role to fill in
the world and is important in some
respect. Everyone, including and perhaps
especially you, is indispensable.

NATHANIEL HAWTHORNE

God gives us all gifts, special abilities that
we are entrusted with developing in order
to help serve Him and serve others.

---

*God has given each of you a gift
from his great variety of spiritual gifts.
Use them well to serve one another.*

1 PETER 4:10 NLT

Unique Gifts

God has a wonderful plan for each person
He has chosen. He knew even before
He created this world what beauty He
would bring forth from our lives.

LOUIS B. WYLY

This is the real gift: you have been given
the breath of life, designed with a unique,
one-of-a-kind soul that exists forever—the
way that you choose to live it doesn't change
the fact that you've been given the gift
of "being," now and forever. Priceless in
value, you are handcrafted by God. He has
a personal design and plan for each of us.

WENDY MOORE

Only God gives true peace—a quiet gift
He sets within us just when we think
we've exhausted our search for it.

God's peace is joy resting. His
joy is peace dancing.

F. F. BRUCE

———————————

*The LORD will give strength
unto his people; the LORD will
bless his people with peace.*

PSALM 29:11 KJV

Footpath to Peace

To be glad of life, because it gives you the
chance to love and to work and to play
and to look up at the stars; to be satisfied
with your possessions, but not contented
with yourself until you have made the
best of them...to think seldom of your
enemies, often of your friends, and every
day of Christ; and to spend as much time
as you can, with body and with spirit
in God's out-of-doors—these are little
guideposts on the footpath to peace.

HENRY VAN DYKE

[Jesus] brings hope, forgiveness, heart
cleansing peace and power. He is
our deliverer and coming King.

LUCILLE M. LAW

By love alone is God enjoyed; by love alone
delighted in, by love alone approached
and admired. His nature requires love.

THOMAS TRAHERNE

Love does not allow lovers
to belong anymore to themselves,
but they belong only to the Beloved.

DIONYSIUS

---

*Love the LORD your God
with all your heart, all your
soul, and all your strength.*

DEUTERONOMY 6:5 NLT

By Love Alone

There is an essential connection between experiencing God, loving God, and trusting God. You will trust God only as much as you love Him, and you will love Him to the extent you have touched Him, rather that He has touched you.

BRENNAN MANNING

Our assurance is not based upon our ability to conjure up some special feeling. Rather, it is built upon a confident assurance in the faithfulness of God. We focus on His trustworthiness and especially on His steadfast love.

RICHARD J. FOSTER

In the presence of hope—faith is
born. In the presence of faith, love
becomes a possibility! In the presence
of love—miracles happen!

ROBERT SCHULLER

Where there is faith, there is love.
Where there is love, there is peace.
Where there is peace, there is God.
Where there is God, there is no need.

_God is able to make all grace
abound to you, so that in all things
at all times, having all that you need,
you will abound in every good work._

2 CORINTHIANS 9:8 NIV

Miracle of Grace

Face your deficiencies and acknowledge
them.... Let them teach you patience,
sweetness, insight. When we do
the best we can, we never know
what miracle is wrought in our
life, or in the life of another.

HELEN KELLER

Hope is some extraordinary spiritual
grace that God gives us to control
our fears, not to oust them.

VINCENT MCNABB

Jesus Christ has brought every need,
every joy, every gratitude, every hope
of ours before God. He accompanies us
and brings us into the presence of God.

DIETRICH BONHOEFFER

The "air" which our souls need also
envelops all of us at all times and
on all sides. God is round about
us...on every hand, with many-
sided and all-sufficient grace.

OLE HALLESBY

---

*My God of mercy shall
come to meet me.*

PSALM 59:10 NKJV

Every Need

God wants nothing from us except
our needs, and these furnish Him with
room to display His bounty when He
supplies them freely.... Not what I have,
but what I do not have, is the first point
of contact between my soul and God.

CHARLES H. SPURGEON

When life becomes difficult, when cracks
spread through our existence and our
strength seems to leak out, fill the gaps
with hope. Like gold adorning distressed
ancient art, hope will reinforce, add
value, and reveal more beauty.

BARBARA FARMER

Love means to love that which is unlovable,
or it is no virtue at all; forgiving means
to pardon that which is unpardonable, or
it is no virtue at all—and to hope means
hoping when things are hopeless,
or it is no virtue at all.

G. K. CHESTERTON

We must strengthen, defend, preserve, and
comfort each other. We must love one another.

JOHN WINTHROP

---

*Dear friends, since God so loved us,
we also ought to love one another.... If
we love one another, God lives in us
and his love is made complete in us.*

1 JOHN 4:11–12 NIV

Love One Another

You who have received so much love share
it with others. Love others the way that
God has loved you, with tenderness.

MOTHER TERESA

Let Jesus be in your heart,
Eternity in your spirit,
The world under your feet,
The will of God in your actions.
And let the love of God shine forth from you.

CATHERINE OF GENOA

Every single act of love bears the imprint of God.

God, who has led you safely on so far,
will lead you on to the end. Be altogether
at rest in the loving holy confidence
which you ought to have in His
heavenly Providence.

FRANCIS DE SALES

God makes a promise—faith believes it, hope
anticipates it, patience quietly awaits it.

---

*The LORD leads with unfailing love
and faithfulness all who keep his covenant
and obey his demands.*

PSALM 25:10 NLT

Faithful Guide

Guidance is a sovereign act. Not merely
does God will to guide us by showing
us His way...whatever mistakes we
may make, we shall come safely home.
Slippings and strayings there will be,
no doubt, but the everlasting arms
are beneath us; we shall be caught,
rescued, restored. This is God's promise;
this is how good He is. And our self-distrust,
while keeping us humble, must not
cloud the joy with which we lean
on our faithful covenant God.

J. I. Packer

To the children of God there stands, behind
all that changes and can change, only
one unchangeable joy. That is God.

HANNAH WHITALL SMITH

Remember, as His precious child,
you are very special to God. He has
promised to complete the good work
He has begun in you. As you continue to
grow in Him, He will make you a
blessing to others.

---

*What marvelous love the Father
has extended to us! Just look at
it—we're called children of God!*

1 JOHN 3:1 *THE MESSAGE*

Child of God

When we call on God, He bends down
His ear to listen, as a father bends
down to listen to his little child.

ELIZABETH CHARLES

He only is the Maker
of all things near and far;
He paints the wayside flower,
He lights the evening star;
the wind and waves obey Him,
by Him the birds are fed;
much more to us, His children,
He gives our daily bread.

MATTHIAS CLAUDIUS

I would maintain that thanks are the highest form of thought, and that gratitude is happiness doubled by wonder.

G. K. CHESTERTON

The love of the Father is like a sudden rain shower that will pour forth when you least expect it, catching you up into wonder and praise.

RICHARD J. FOSTER

I will give thanks to the LORD with all my heart; I will tell of all Your wonders. I will be glad and exult in You; I will sing praise to Your name, O Most High.

PSALM 9:1–2 NASB

Source of Wonder

Dear Lord, grant me the grace of wonder.
Surprise me, amaze me, awe me in every
crevice of your universe.... Each day enrapture
me with your marvelous things without
number. I do not ask to see the reason for it
all; I ask only to share the wonder of it all.

Joshua Abraham Heschel

May our lives be illumined
by the steady radiance
renewed daily,
of a wonder,
the source of which
is beyond reason.

Dag Hammarskjöld

Hope sees the invisible, feels the intangible,
and achieves the impossible.

When all my plans and hopes
are fading like a shadow,
when all my dreams lie crumbled at my feet,
I will look up and know the night
will bring tomorrow,
and that my Lord will bring me what I need.

GLORIA GAITHER

I pray also that the eyes of your heart
may be enlightened in order that you may
know the hope to which he has called you.

EPHESIANS 1:18 NIV